In the
Boarding House for
Unclaimed Girls

Also by Toni Thomas:

Chosen
    Brick Road Poetry Press

Fast as Lightening
    Gribble Press

Walking on Water
    Finishing Line Press

Blue Halo
    Annalese Press

Ace Raider of the Unfathomable Universe
    Annalese Press

You'll be Fast as Lightning Coveting my Painted Tail
    Annalese Press

Hotsy Totsy Ballroom
    Annalese Press

Love Adrift in the City of Stars
    Annalese Press

In the Pink Arms of the City
    Annalese Press

In the Kingdom of Longing
    Annalese Press

The Things We Don't Know
    Annalese Press

In the Boarding House for Unclaimed Girls

Poems

First published in 2021 by Annalese Press
134 Towngate
Netherthong
Holmfirth
West Yorkshire HD9 3XZ
England

Copyright © 2021 Toni Thomas

Please Note
All characters and situations appearing
in these pages are in the service of poetry.
Any resemblance to real persons,
living or dead, is purely coincidental.

All rights reserved. No part of this publication may be reproduced, stored, or transmitted in any form, or by any means electronic, mechanical or photo-copying, recording or otherwise, without the express written permission of the publisher.

Cover design and illustrations by
Peter Wadsworth
Lucy Madox Brown by Ford Madox Brown

British Library Cataloguing-in-Publication Data
A catalogue record for this book is available on request from the British Library.

ISBN 978-1-9163620-2-4

Contents

EPIGRAPH

PART ONE: *Unclaimed*

Out of our house ached an epiphany	3
In the shoplifter's paradise	4
I finger the emerald scarf	5
I am the courteous shopper	6
Inside the girl's hiss fit	7
Out of our house	8
In the boarding house for unclaimed girls	9
And what do you know	10
Some people	11
The girl dines on apologies	12
Who unbraids	13
Some of us	14
In July	15
You are crushing ants	16
Are you hungry like me?	17
Not everyone lives on empty	18
Sometimes my words	19

PART TWO: *In the photograph*

Mama warns us	23
In the photograph	24
My father is going away	25
The day holds foam and waves	26
When the wave comes in jump	27
Looking at this picture	28
We cup our hands	29

I sit on the steps	30
Very soon	31
In the newspaper the man sipping wine	32
When you carry the suitcases of the dead	33
We table hope	34
We collect food coupons	35
I will not trouble you	36
In the photograph death is a disguised thing	37
In the casket	38
First I was passed	39
Back then	40

PART THREE: *Restless*

In the boarding house	45
We catalog folktales	46
The immaculate bride	47
I calculated a thorn bush	48
I am the tease in a blue dress	49
The man down the road	50
A hover queen	51
Heinrich the cat	52
Summer spills into autumn	53
We became Christmas	54
We hang hosiery	55
There were sleepless nights	56
Out in the field	57
No one gave us	58
What did we know	59

PART FOUR: *The Suitcases of the Dead*

We coaxed our swear words	63
You puddle the fried egg	64
Spring arrives fisted with rain	65
My mother wanted her casket closed	66
I want to scout	67
I have come this far	68
I don't want to believe anymore	69
He is not the one who listens	70
It is not easy	71
Someday you will find me	72
In the garden	73

PART FIVE: *To Hold a Rare Bird*

In the hotel	77
In the valley	78
Beyond the spotted hills	79
You scratch my words	80
My love for you	81
Make me	82
You mythologize fear	83
I build a nest of sorts	84
Not all stories proceed in mayhem	85
See how I finger	86
September	87
I have given up fasting	88
You place rice in my shoes	89
I walk with you by the river	90
In the boarding house for wreckless girls	91

*What shall I do singer and first-born
in a world where the deepest black is grey
and inspiration is kept in a thermos?
With all this immensity
in a measured world?*

Marina Tsvetaeva

PART ONE

Unclaimed

Out of our house ached an epiphany

asphyxiation wore a blue veil
but that was years ago
when the trees forgot my name
animals went unattended

when sunlight dimpled the surface of the lake
my mother jumped off the dock
in her short shorts
reckless

when my size was no asset or defect
and every season sped toward summer
like an anxious wind.

Over time I learned
to serve plums
from a pearled plate.
It was not difficult.
The birds called my name
men came and went as lovers.

How would you
console yourself
what would you do
if the seasons
of your life
went missing?

In the shoplifter's paradise

there are racks of mink
spike heels, cashmere
designer slacks that lift off the shelf
anxious to find me.

The security guard dreams pot-roast
the sales lady in hosiery
hovers over the dark haired woman
with spider veined legs.

See how I finger the dress from Dior
its pearl stippled neck, scarlet trim
as if it whispers lonely

stuff you in my bag
sinful.

I finger the emerald scarf

help it slide off the shelf
into my purse

plump my voice blonde
learn to consolidate
wipe my ass with a soiled doily
live on mac and cheese
breadsticks

navigate the past
bury the blue soldier

watch you
manhandle the snow

impervious.

I am the courteous shopper

in pert leather boots, navy coat
finger blouses
unruly ones
that slip off the hanger
beg to be pawed

finger men
peonies, pens
the fur of rabbits
surface of the moon unfettered
won't be easily subdued
somebody else's rollover.

Out on the street
you make the sign of the cross
as if it means something
health for the eldest daughter
willing hectares of land
placards for the deceased
good fortune on the
forehead of newlyweds
remedy for the sick cow.

I am the courteous shopper
carry suitcases nobody sees
wish lists and lament
sodden apostrophes
don't want things to go missing
be the axed field
unheard contrition
take your body
fondle it in my hands
greedy.

Inside the girl's hiss fit

the dark is no stranger
the territory of want
hangs on nails
June stapled to lilac
the scrum of mahogany boats
bobbing on steel grey waves
out in the bay.

The girl has a jar, rice
remembers the words of Dako
the territory of greed is a blind mule
isn't sure how to save things
call luck back
into the arms of strangers.

Does something thread
through the girl's life
thicker than a prayer book
fish limp bodies out of the river
unbind the dead
answer her night field
with a flood of rabbits?

Out of our house

sped swallows, plovers
the night's thin veil.
We promised to be faithful
more than a salvaged word
uneven sunset.

It was before the pert face
circumcision of boys
condemnation of mice
when even Schrodinger's cat
was destined for a decent life
beyond peril

nothing was condemned
a cat both dead and alive
provisional.

In the boarding house for unclaimed girls

we learn to consolidate
flirt with scarcity
the half-baked field
road kill
refuse the spotless bride
pay as you go summer

nail the wind
to keep the sermon of leaves
from fleeing.

Tell me –
when autumn casts her dark net
who will call our name
as holy
as if we are more than
the marooned rope
shelved prophecy?

And what do you know

of hard circumstance
the ragged yard
tainted sunset

what do you know
about trespass
the shattered dress
men who wedge
their way in
not generous
fluid as the river
but spiteful?

Some people

must cradle the dark
hypnotize want
siren a love
that is never easy.

When I was a child
did the tiny sailboats
on my one piece swimsuit
speak

where did they want
to travel me to
what did they say?

The girl dines on apologies

waits like a porcelain vase
for the hour of roses
wants to save things
fish limp bodies out of the river.

If she listens
will the suitcases of the dead
turn weightless

speak more than guttural
turn her thin dress
into a prayer
of snow?

Who unbraids

the man's forehead
soothes the field
readies it for lovers
their white bodies radiant
after the rain

who tames the waves
makes them behave

travels me as I swim
takes me to exotic places

never clip, clip, clips
till I am a mute shell
voiceless?

Some of us

walk through
corridors of conceit
shoeless
want to marry thin circumstance
be more than the blind mule
fact list
truncated summer.

Can an ocean
hold the whole world
in the guise a blue swimsuit
do the bell jars of the dead
sing?

In July

the heat melts plastic
turns stray cats
into shade

we sweep crumbs
put cloth over the bread, apples
keep flies distant

in the cramped courtyard
pin socks, panties, skirts
to the line
listen.

You are crushing ants

want to rid the world
of kitchen colonies
shelf climbers
sugar fiends.

And I wonder about
our future
homeless girls
without a stake in the world
always pining for something
just beyond our reach

too scant a voice
needy to feed
tomorrow's extermination
or the next?

Are you hungry like me

please bring the bread
my rosebuds are a city of tears
my garland your crucifixion.

It is late.
Why do you leave me waiting?

Not everyone lives on empty

some of us
carry the jars of the dead
lip read loss
practice a silence
more sonorous
than bread

are spring flowers
in want of home.

When I come to you
may it be as
a ceremony of roses.

Sometimes my words

are more yours than mine.
You fill me.
You fill me.
The afternoon swells with heat
small winged creatures
blackberries
fevered lovemaking.

I promise to be faithful.

Part Two

In the Photograph

Mama warns us

the ocean can swallow
be careful
so we stay in close amid
blobs of jellyfish, seaweed.
My one piece swimsuit is navy
hosts a slew of sailboats
that want to travel me.

Up on the blanket
my mama's body is copper sheened
muscular and perfect.
She laughs with her friend.

You might think looking at the photograph
my mama watches me
will teach me how to swim
doesn't care much about
her packed away paintings
mothballed gowns
doesn't care my father's heart
is an orphaned wing.

You might think
wolves stay confined to a storybook
birds climb into my soul
deathless.

In the photograph

I am in the too small one piece swimsuit
chubby, the watcher of children
you can't tell I am afraid of the waves
the sting of jellyfish

my mother is a valley of smooth curves
sermons the sea
ensures nothing goes missing

in the photograph
I appear careful, willing
no harbor of a sad boat
the waves call my name
shells refuse to get crippled
the light torches

in the photograph
everything looks possible
we guzzle pop
seize summer with our bare fists.

My father is going away

has always been going away
but now it is certain
no more jokes
boxes of crayons
promises
he cannot keep.

I have grown used to him this way
provisional
an apostrophe waiting
grown used to his nearly departed
not really here
never enough.

Tell me then – what will the world
become without him
who will call my name
kiss then scratch
heave their might
across my body
cripple my voice
heavy as a truck?

The day holds foam and waves

the promise of salami sandwiches
chips, Koolaid.
We have our hair pinned up in double braids
don't worry about our once lifeguard mother
her perfectly muscled arms
know in a moment's flash she can save us

keep our worry for the man
who will never appear in our photographs
the one we've been told to forget
who mama says *needs to be other places*
sends birthday cards and candy
whose legs are as long as a spider
whose hands hold card tricks and coin.

We are splashing in the waves
splash splash splash
too young to know about the newspaper
the man sipping Pinot Gris
at the Flamingo Bar in L.A.
what he is about to do
what he will take from us.

When the wave comes in *jump*

but my little sister says *I don't want to.*
I'm holding her hand
supposed to look after her.
She hates getting her feet wet.
Up the sand mama is laughing
her body slender, bronzed
in the skimpy swimsuit.

Lunchtime she unfolds
the wax papered sandwiches
warns I look chubby
the devils food cake in the cooler
is not for me.

I want to splash
soak my arms, legs, hair
in the salt water
travel the world
lithe as a fish.

Looking at this picture

you might think I get to choose
my own swimsuit
not the sappy one piece
that makes my legs look big
but something turquoise, slimming
sublime.

You might think the child
whose hand I am holding
is my favorite
but she is not
she's my cry baby little sister
and I have no choice but to watch her

might think I enjoy being the oldest
always responsible
have been taught how to swim
claim things
go out in the water not drown

that over time my body will never
whittle itself down
thin as a twig.

We cup our hands

want to cradle the next wave
the starfish that nobody sees.

In the photograph everything is foam
the promise of cake
a float tube.

I paint my hands white
am too young to know
I won't be able to save my mother
that no man wants a woman
with crimped wings.

I sit on the steps

of the three family house
hope for a friend.

No one knows the worms
of the dark have invaded me
death wears a blue veil.

Who will unscrew this sorrow
that turns in my head
heavy as a crushed toy?

It is mid-June.
time of the bees' foraging
hope that wears painted nails
a propped swimsuit.

Very soon

my father will no longer
read a newspaper
watch the late night news
move from kitchen to couch
crack eggs, fry pancake

very soon he won't be the man
who sends birthday cards
boxes of chocolate
claims he'll come back.

My mother will take a new suitor
kiss the death out of him
claim we are snot nosed kids
ungrateful
that the life ahead of her
was always meant to be
a vat of gems

very soon I'll be labeled *unteachable*
the girl who minds no manners
knows no fork
forgets how to speak

sent off to this other place
where birds fly in my ear
every day is thin boned
uneventful.

In the newspaper the man sipping wine

shows no sign of a weapon
nothing says he is my father
that behind his aviator sunglasses
some important part of his life
has gone missing

that he will do terrible things
he may or may not someday regret.

No one visibly places
a stake in my heart
the porters of the dead
are missing

but still this weight
curves my back

still I have become
the fallen girl
speck of dust
amid platinum.

When you carry the suitcases of the dead

you cannot assume things
that money calms a fever
memories are a prayer book
my nightdress carries wings
the scrum of the dark speaks loyal.

Some seasons are skeletal.
Apparitions arrive shoeless.

Tell me –
can scarcity spawn a glass eye
the ocean hold a bold world
in the guise of a blue swimsuit?

We tabled hope

slammed it like a ping pong ball
back and forth
back and forth
over the net.

My mama called us damaged children.

Every day the sky turned
the moon wanton
birds whimpered

we lit candles
called them scrap prayer
a meal ticket

I scrubbed out my mouth
so it could carry
your butter and rain.

We collect food coupons

stamps
recognize there are no guarantees
the night chucks up hairballs
things happen
ask us to be more than
the blind ball player
complacent.

Very soon my father
will not remember which shoe
goes on which foot
where the canned soup gets kept
why his blue shirt is missing

will not remember
which way to the bathroom
how his trailer key turns
what color my hair is
the month I was born

will not remember
the way my body
whittled itself down so small
he couldn't snap it
with the might of his fist.

I will not trouble you

with my sorrows
that are one part soured fruit
a stolen ocean

believe god
is a field of lemons
slice them in half
suck out the juice

paint my hands white
as a communion dress.

Am too young to know
decency hangs on a thin thread
I won't be able to save things

no man wants a girl
with crimped wings.

In the photograph death is a disguised thing

holds no gun
I am the girl in the swimsuit
come and go
come and go
uncontaminated

in the photograph
the sea is benign, does not gobble
every wave I encounter
is tickle and tease
the foam of the light's perfect halter

in the photograph he sends me
pop up cards, candy
the newspaper headlines stay fiction

the man sipping wine at the bar in L.A.
would never go beserk
carry a weapon.

In the casket

my father has skin caked grey
hair slicked down
hard as a Kansas heatwave.
My mother refuses to look
afterwards paints her hair red
stamps hope into a new passport.

Later many miles from me
her pencil sketches faded
the dog dying of loneliness in the yard
my mother will drop her morning teacup
onto the kitchen floor, die.

And as for me
no showy bloom in a field of Aprils
I will stump trellis my life
wear my robes nameless
the squat breeze
in a secret meadow.

First I was passed

to the Italian neighbors with three kids
but they said I was needy
then onto my aunt's house in Buffalo
place where the snow buries cars, big hedges
where you get smacked
for not saying your *please* and *thank yous*
where I was labeled impudent
the truant girl in a sea of laundry
till finally I was sent here
to the boarding school for restless girls
place where they promise to put things right
turn us into well-mannered candy.

You might think I've learned not to fuss
about the state of the world, injustice
have become the model citizen
docile napkin
till you look inside close
hear the rasp of my voice
blue of my heart's bleeding.

Back then

our photographs
held a blue cooler, plastic tumblers
beach tubes and cake
two girls in look-a-like braids
held my navy swimsuit
sun and sand
a mother whose eyes
mirror imaged the ocean.

Now every member of my family
has become a bloodied river
blue host
the world carries
my name not as salt
but gypsum.

Where can I go?

Part Three

Restless

In the boarding house

we dine on fry bread
the clock's insistence
weather that tantrums the dark
holds the spotless bride hostage

learn to consolidate
wipe our ass with newspaper
nail the wind down
to keep the sermon of leaves
from emptying.

I cellophane want
poke holes in my prayer book
stock up on cans of soup, peaches
unanchored boys
help them become more than
the thin field
faithless meadow.

We catalog folktales

memorize wolves
girls slipped under the ice
the rare marbled egg
deathless nightingale

want to believe no past can bind
we will forever worship
the intricacy of snowflakes.

We are iodine and lace
the rusted voice, camouflage.
Boys run after us
rip through the field
till the ferns bleed.

The immaculate bride

doesn't live here
nor the reclusive one
damped down shrine of roses

folks fear me
put my name in their grisly
draw sticks over what will happen
as if I am a maimed creature
peep show

but then what do they know
about endurance
scavenger winter
god thrashing amid the bed sheets

what do they know
of the mucked up lake
love toyed and yanked
hard as a fish hook?

I calculated a thorn bush

then a rose tree
calculated three fists of corn
a brick oven for bad wolves
calculated hope and hearsay
soiled gloves
a box car of mercy

calculated thunder
till my mind grew muscular
spit at the dark
threatened to gobble the porridge
melt ice
tipster a brandy

till even the soup in my bowl
couldn't be trusted
without first measuring the peas.

I am the tease in a blue dress

thick eye liner
float a hem of lace
inside the bane of winter

drink the dark down
till it turns literate
a winsome girl
in a navy coat
the one who wakes early
whisks egg, burns toast
feeds desolate birds
a host of suet.

In our dorm room spiders
climb out of nowhere
walk the ceiling
black as the color of death.
I am afraid they will descend
take my longing and strangle.

On Saturdays we clutch stick bats
send a ball across the neighbor's fence
where the boy in the yellow house lives
the one I make believe doesn't love me
make believe will never send me
an anonymous vase of roses
snatch up my disbelief
show me his forest.

The man down the road

burnt himself to death a month ago
after his wife disappeared.
A can of kerosene, too many matches.
It was gruesome.

And I wonder about the ashen
remains of his house
the family photograph albums
boxed Christmas
teacups and doilies
stained couch
clothes his wife once wore
her chiffon scarf, purple pantsuit

did they smolder slow
or in one fell swoop
ignite?

A hover queen

doesn't peril her wingspan
let you mess with the rudder
snatch secrets

pays attention to thermals
the wind's casual or caustic
the night's habit of swiping

learns to navigate
travel the forensic sunset

make you behave
not loot her body
with your boney fingers.

Heinrich the cat

used to prefer kippers
a good doze till teatime
but that was before the commissary
of orphaned books set in.

Now he dons wire glasses
stays up all hours
contemplating Nietzsche
the place beyond good and evil
fans the deck
for our nurses' nightly game
of rummy.

All evening Heinrich the cat
deals out cards
watchs birds climb into my soul
thick as honey
speechless

watches cracks in the sky loosen
the wolves pace
hungry.

Summer spills into autumn

hummingbirds flit
tree to plant to feeder
sip then vanish
like the man who comes
out of nowhere
thirsty
arrives at my body's ruby orb
insists

but I don't want him to pass
his barbed tongue over me
make my life a beggar
need to sing for my meals
in only his voice
his avenue of conquests.

We became Christmas

Hanukkah and Lenten
became the headmaster's shrill stick
parrot's mimic
icebergs and a slut dance
learned to eat with a bent fork
accept the bruised end
of the meatloaf.

I grew my hair long
trained my limp
till nobody noticed

called you my desolate angel
the one who busts things
secretly glues them back.

We hang hosiery

pin panties and pale blouses
want January to behave
the men out on the lake ice fishing
to notice our shapely legs
season of pudding

want what the world wants
and lots of it
play vacations in the sun
lobster and mango
a kiss feast

want to be squeezed
spill our river of juice
all over you
shameless.

There were sleepless nights

dogs barking
bunk beds with iced sheets
but still we were willing

fire stirred in our chests
the night spoke fine boned syllables
animals grew wild and peckish.

I etched your name in the dust
ate the cakes of the dead
called them *good*
came to you a flirtive season
in a dwarf landscape

glossed my hair, my lips
begged to become more than
the kingdom of cheese sandwiches

shameless
brave.

Out in the field

we search stray dogs
nobody wants

they are fur mangled
surplus to the world's needs
eat our scrap
bed in the bushes
learn *come sit stay*
lift your paw
do not resist
shore up resentment

sponge my hands, my face
for free
like god.

No one gave us

a Christmas of wrapped boxes
fruitcake

no one carved our name in the tree
troubadoured love songs
spat at the room for not hosting.

Tides accumulated
winter slit my purse
into a series of ice storms.

You cropped the tail of my cat
determined to teach me manners
spent nothing of your inheritance
to help me see.

What did we know

about fast cars
fast roads
fast boys with their hand
on the gears
life beyond the gate?

We were young when we were taken
not Pollyannas
not polished as heirloom silver
just knobby legs and a pinched voice.

Was it for lack of love we arrived here
because the tuitions of the world fail
turn unwieldy

or just that someone fell and then another
someone knelt and then another

till we became driftwood
ordinary and porous
fallen gods without a wing?

Part Four

The Suitcases of the Dead

We coaxed our swear words

to calm down
sound no trumpets
shhhh we told them *shhhh*
coaxed our shoes to *rest slow*
rest slow
our wants to not riot

called down the birds
the rosemary
night's somnolence

as if the dark holds jewels
beyond the weeping
something cradles us
bestows

things come apart
can rise up again
tender
beautiful.

You puddle the fried egg

on my toast
grind lust
lick the commotion of roses

wait for me to be more than
the bent trellis
cat that pees on the sofa

wait for the ice to clear
my mind to unman winter.

Spring arrives fisted with rain

orange petals of poppy
spilt across concrete.
I retrace my life
as if what we become
is more than the shriveled rose
sun's eclipse.

Back then what did I promise
a lithe thing oblivious to stings

every meadow called my name
the day never felt burdened
with theory.

My mother wanted her casket closed

so we wouldn't witness
the unsung lines of her face
would succor the living
instead of the dead.

Death hurts
even when it's a stranger
you find lifeless
lying in a pickup truck
off a dirt road.

But then I am familiar
with the suitcases of the dead
their parlor talk
slatted shoes
sermon of loose ends

as if even the runt voice
pelted swimsuit
has a story

can hold the waters
of the world
in a single gulp.

I want to scout

for heaven
from a sturdy pole
make my words
not veiled slats
of a siren hotel
but durable

able to rid
the trumpet flower
of poison
will back
the swan infused lake

fine the shy woodsman
who never slanders
a woman's body
takes her leaf kingdom
and rakes.

I have come this far

and still the porters
are missing
still the weight of the dead
curves my back
till I am a small thing
speck of dust
in a sea of unctuous.

Tell me –
if I cried out
in the city of angels
who would hear me
hold me to their heart
as if I am more than
blue terror
pestilence?

I don't want to believe anymore

that you are a grove
of shrunken lemons
suicidal
when the blade cuts

or bitter as a raven

don't want to believe
everyone I ever loved disappears
that I am the girl
of orphaned circumstance
no mother, father
sister, bride

but then
you can live forever
with a shrunken wing.

Somebody once told me that.
Is it true?

He is not the one who listens

plants a worm in my chest
corrugates summer till it folds

but will anyone suspect
I am more than the debunked field
corn gone rancid

over time
will sip the cup of his gall
turn it into a fruit tree.

It is not easy

being orphaned
at a young age

made to hunt
down kisses

turn bird kill
into a meal

mine the dark
of its suet

but still
things are meant
to come right

cradle the earth
abide
by better vows

so I take the heel
of the bread

nurse it
into daydreams.

Someday you will find me

not as Rapunzel up in the watch tower
my river of red hair twined
into a rope line

not stirring mace into the jam jar
rearranging the matchsticks

watering only the geraniums
while the moon stays thirsty

but durable
easy on the eyes

my distances outrun
my wants small.

See how I will run to you
unimpaired

unbutton my blouse
call you my first, my only

swollen sooth of nightingale.

In the garden

death hums
thick
as a pageant

wind rips
through the iris
the stray dog
barks
night vexes
the roses.

In the garden
I wait
shy glint
of the eye's apostles
lotus blossom
after the rain.

Part Five

To Hold a Rare Bird

In the hotel

we clutch bird plates
duck spoons
a ceramic pig

vessels that marry beaver
dog, beetle, fox
tether to fresh linen days
meadow.

The spring water is flecked
with pine needles
wash your face and they tickle

hold your hand out
a nob of bread appears

open your lunchbox
to a sea of gherkins.

Maybe some folks believe
scarcity breeds a barbed fence
but I am the lost cousin
of the Dowager of Plenty
watch how for me
the tides roll in an orchestra
fish dance.

In the valley

where the one I love
salts the bread, tomatoes
drags bushels of rye
might pass as a marooned treatise

in the township heavy
with hazelnuts
women who tattoo their wrists
to sagas of wind
moonlight

in the valley
where love waits
the sycamore swoons
elegies float
above the meadow

a young girl can be struck dumb
blind
forget her name
occupation
history.

Beyond the spotted hills

plates of sardine and thistle
truncated versions of love
that wear barbed feet
beyond hope
the garden immaculate
the surreptitious and masterly

beyond the crooked fist
smashed hole in the moon's mantle
pearly teeth, elocution
beyond the three tier cake
genocide and tent cities
money's fornication
beyond reason and fortitude
vengeance and rumination
I call to you

not just because the world leaks
plastic goodness won't save me
but because my mother's absence
must count for something
my sister's heart failure had a cause
because my father rises on stilts
to keep his past from blazing
because not all things come right
not all things come right
because the child inside this woman
needs to hear the balm
of your singing.

You scratch my words

across sandpaper
saga the lily
repair the roof's shingle
turn the rain from pelt
into river

when my empty plate
begs at your table

answer with feast.

My love for you

is five measures hope
a cemetery of lost birds

my love for you
is a torn sunset
one orchid
window lace that refuses to sleep.

January wears a cross
the neighbors carry
in their voices' chain link.
Snow drifts bury the porch
hold the house hostage.

I offer up bread
seedy jam
sponge my body
inside the wet penitentiary
of your lips.

Make me

supplicate as the sea to her tides
the stars to the moon's mantle
the wind to the sky's bedtime

make me more than
my clipped vision of midnight
chrome shoes
more than paradise on a pole stick
the esplanade buried in pickpockets

make me
in the least of my counterfeits
the onion field
that burns your midnight
the thankful tree
come cry of pheasant.

You mythologize fear

mortar the sun
shave down my legs
slide want into a slush cone.

See how my dorm bed lifts
the warden gifts us with butter
the ragged clothes of the past
turn tweed

see how I eat wormed apples
rename them star fruit
kiss death as it flies
turn ordinary broth
into syrup.

See how the earth
gets canonized
the spindly azalea
turn monumental
in moonlight.

I build a nest of sorts

stick gum and rush
wax and mace
birch twigs
twine them together
make a house
softer than the tongues of men
who want to carry my body off
then migrate

proclaim you
my everlasting
newborn bride
hoist you up
inside the sun's halo.

Not all stories proceed in mayhem

become barbed words
the slit throat.

Sometimes a girl spits out
the Shrove Tuesday
on her tongue

learns to listen
set up a deathbed
not as mortuary
but vacant plot

welcomes
the stray dandelions
weeds
dearly departed

becomes
a repository
for truant roses.

See how I finger

the soft curve of your cheek
as if it whispers lonely
slide my body next to you in the car
offer up my low cut dress
cider and poems.

See how out of my house
leaks an epiphany.

Tell me –
when the summers of your life
go missing
will you rediscover me
find the gem
in a sea of thread?

September

wind in the trees
the field speckled with the last
of the dwarf melon
shingles curled on the roof
like a lifted dress.
Up the road
a valley of clear-cuts.

On the tip of my tongue
just this one word –
stay.

I have given up fasting

turning what was once feast
into famine's nameplate

given up sideways glances
men who talk smart
while the world weeps

given up the ambition
for one of a kind
designer dresses
unapologetic books

want to hold
this strange bird
in my palm
not flinch
run away.

You place rice in my shoes

for good luck you say
and for the seasons
flushed with rain
the peril of poppies

don't say the world traffics in greed
things gets stolen
just place rice in my shoes
mix with a bit of spit
sugar.

Outside in the yard
socks and panties marry the sun
the neighbor child shakes down
wormed apples
turns them holy.

I walk with you by the river

sometimes my words are more yours
than my own.
You fill me. You fill me.
The afternoon swells with heat
small winged creatures
blackberries
last night's fevered lovemaking

and in your eyes
I see the brown hills
mottled with trees
the furrow of donkeys
the sky unafraid to empty
sun after the rain
witness the amber candles
icons of Mary.

See how stereophonic the future leans
the past gives up its landmines
how out of the slant corner
of your eye
my wounded bird sings.

In the boarding house for wreckless girls

I stomp across the cobbles
in my provocative
that never runs smooth
is more than seersucker cute
a tempting éclair.

See how I finger the linden tree
as if it whispers lonely
learn to consolidate
tag my life to an ancient bird

see how I refuse
the spotless bride
pay as you go sunset

become fur eclipsed
shiny as seal skin

traipse through your fields
attempt to carry my cross
weightless.

Toni Thomas lives in Portland, Oregon. Her poems have been published in Austria, Spain, New Zealand, Canada, England, Scotland, and Australia. In the United States her work has appeared in over fifty literary magazines including *Prairie Schooner, North Dakota Quarterly, Hayden's Ferry Review, the Minnesota Review, Notre Dame Review, Poetry East*, and more. She has been twice nominated for a Pushcart prize, and won several awards. She has published ten collections of poetry and two books for children.

Her figurative clay sculptures have been shown in gallery exhibits in Portland and Chicago, displayed in literary magazines, and housed in private collections in the U.S. and England.

Her short documentary *One of Us* was shown at the Trans-ideology: Nostalgia festival in Berlin and at the Museum of Contemporary Art in Taipei.

Since Toni loves to create and sits buried in reams of poems, manuscripts, clay figures and images….she likes to imagine all of them out in the world, swaying wild as the lupine.

tonithomaspoetry.com

www.ingramcontent.com/pod-product-compliance
Lightning Source LLC
Chambersburg PA
CBHW021444080526
44588CB00009B/677